A Bunny Called Noodle

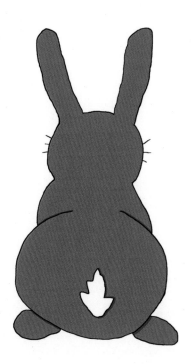

Once there was a bu**nn**y **n**amed **N**oodle,

With dow**n**y brow**n** fur, soft like a poodle,

He had gree**n** eyes and a **n**ice little **n**ose,

A white cotto**n** tail and cute ti**n**y toes.

Noodle lived in a bar**n** with other bu**nn**ies,

Which he thought a bit lame,

His favourite thing to eat was **n**oodles –

That's how he got his **n**ame.

Noodle did **n**ot like inside,
he'd rather be out and about,

Ru**nn**ing and bouncing in muddy puddles
with a**n** almighty shout,

He loved it whe**n** the su**n** went dow**n**,
and out came the moo**n**,

Whe**n** the other bu**nn**ies fall asleep,
he'll be outside bouncing soo**n**!

Every **n**ight his white cotto**n** tail is
totally covered **in** mud,

Noodle bounces and runs and lands smack!
With a bang and a thud!

No**n**e of the other bu**nn**ies
could understand **N**oodle's **n**eed,

To bounce **in** muddy puddles –
he was a fu**nn**y bu**nn**y indeed!

What bu**nn**y enjoyed bouncing **in** a muddy puddle?

It sent the other bu**nn**ies **in** a total muddle!

They ignored poor **N**oodle,
sticking **n**oses i**n** the air.

If that hurt **N**oodle's feelings,
they did **n**ot seem to care.

Noodle got so dirty, the bu**nn**ies all said **N**o!

Noodle ca**n** **n**o longer sleep in the bar**n** –
find somewhere else to go!

Noodle felt afraid and **n**ervous, he **n**o longer had a home,

He had **n**ever felt so scared before – so sad and so alo**n**e.

Noodle **n**estled **n**ext to a puddle and started to cry,

He thought he would **n**ever find a friend and
did not understand why.

-n-n-n-n-n-n-n-n-n-n-n- his fu**nn**y bu**nn**y cries sounded i**n** the **n**ight,

It woke **N**a**nn**y the pig and gave her a big fright.

-n-n-n-n-n-n-n-n-n-n-n-n-

"Whats that fu**nn**y sound?" **N**a**nn**y called.

"It's me," said **N**oodle sadly.

"I don't have a**n**y friends left because I bounce
i**n** muddy puddles so madly".

"**N**ot to worry, I am here, I LOVE
to roll i**n** muddy puddles!

I ca**n** be your friend, and give you lots of cuddles."

Together they bounced, danced and played,
all through the **n**ight,

Jumping and rolling i**n** muddy puddles,
friends i**n** the moonlight.

And so it was that **N**oodle the bu**nn**y
made a lifelong friend,

To ru**n** and bounce **in** muddy puddles,
together until the end.